Loto Cymraeg

A Fun Way to Reinforce Welsh Vocabulary
Ffordd hwyliog o atgyfnerthu geirfa Gymraeg

Colette Elliott and Martin Gwynedd

Brilliant
PUBLICATIONS

We hope you and your pupils enjoy playing the lotto games in this book. Brilliant Publications publishes some other books for teaching in Welsh schools. To find out more details on any of the titles listed below, please log onto our website: www.brilliantpublications.co.uk.

100+ Fun Ideas for Practising Modern Foreign Languages in the Primary Classroom	978-1-903853-98-6
Gêm i Gloi	978-1-905780-16-7
Sut i Ddisgleirio mewn Cyfrif hyd at 10	978-1-903853-41-2
Sut i Ddisgleirio mewn Bondiau Rhif	978-1-903853-43-6
Sut i Ddisgleirio mewn Adio a Thynnu hyd at 20	978-1-903853-40-5
Sut i Ddisgleirio mewn Dechrau Lluosi a Rhannu	978-1-903853-42-9
Sut i Ddisgleirio a Chael Hwyl mewn Mathemateg	978-0-85747-226-7
Sut i Loywi mewn Rhifyddeg Pen	978-0-85747-224-3
Sut i Ddisgleirio mewn Archwiliadau Gwyddoniaeth	978-0-85747-222-9
Sut i Loywi Adeg y Nadolig	978-0-85747-220-5

Published by Brilliant Publications Limited
Unit 10
Sparrow Hall Farm
Edlesborough
Dunstable
Bedfordshire
LU6 2ES, UK

Website: www.brilliantpublications.co.uk

General information enquiries:
Tel: 01525 222292

The name Brilliant Publications and the logo are registered trademarks.

Written by Colette Elliott and Martin Gwynedd
Illustrated by Gaynor Berry
Front cover designed by Brilliant Publications

ISBN 978-1-905780-50-1

First printed and published in the UK in 2009

Contents

Introduction

The perennially popular game of lotto (or 'loto' as it is called in Welsh) is an enjoyable and effective way to teach and/or reinforce vocabulary and language structures. It can be used as a teaching tool or as a fun follow-up activity after a lesson. It provides a stimulating and meaningful way to develop reading, listening and speaking skills.

The games in *Loto Cymraeg* can be played in a variety of ways (see pages 5–7) and with very little preparation from you. There is no need to give the children counters or individual cards. Simply photocopy the boards, hand them out to your pupils together with some colouring pencils and, bingo, you can start playing!

Our unique call sheets provide the 'order of call' and enable you to follow the game closely and to select which team you want to win.

Lotto can be played in small groups, or with an entire class. There is no limit to the number of players and the games are suitable for ages four upwards.

There are seven topics in *Loto Cymraeg*:
- Rhifau 1 i 12   Numbers 1–12
- Rhifau 1 i 60   Numbers 1–60
- Anifeiliaid   Animals
- Bwyd   Food
- Offer ysgol   School equipment
- Dillad   Clothes
- Nadolig   Christmas

For each topic there are three versions of the boards, allowing maximum flexibility, particularly in mixed ability classes.

| **pictures only** | **words and pictures** | **words only** |

The ideas in this book are by no means exhaustive and, should you decide to cut the boards to make flashcards or playing cards, then the number of games is unlimited!

Have fun playing!

How to play

Getting started

For each topic, in each format, there are four different numbered boards, so you can play with four teams. Just photocopy the sheets, cut them in half, and hand out the boards to the children. For a class of 28 pupils, you only need to copy two pages seven times each.

It is a good idea to go through the vocabulary with the children before playing. The best way to do this is either to scan and place the four boards on the whiteboard, or enlarge the 12 pictures on the photocopier and use them as flashcards.

Make sure that the boards are evenly distributed throughout the class. After giving the boards out and before you start playing, ask for a show of hands to see how the teams are spread out in the classroom. The children like to see who is in their team and this increases the element of competition!

How to play

Each topic contains a call sheet, with the words numbered 1 to 12. The caller can start calling from any number. The white area in the table indicates who the winning board will be.

The children can play on their own or in pairs for moral support.

The winner is the first child to shout 'loto' (hopefully the rest of that team will also shout 'loto', but the real winner is the child who shouts out first). Get the winner to say all the words in Welsh whilst you check on the list. This is a good reading/speaking exercise.

Once the first team has won, you can stop the game or carry on until everyone has shouted 'loto' (you will know from the call sheet who the next winner will be).

You can play several games with the same boards by marking the boards in different ways:
◆ Colour the box outline (or only one side of the box if you want to make it last!)
◆ Colour the picture
◆ Colour the background
◆ Tick or cross the box, etc.

It is best to tell the children to shout 'loto' as soon as the caller says the word, rather than wait until the colouring is done, to avoid any arguments.

Variations

Instead of evenly distributing the boards, you could make it a competition within the class: divide the class into four groups, give the same boards to each group, and see which group says 'loto' first.

Children could play in groups of five. One child is the caller (give him/her a photocopy of the call list) and the others use four different boards. Only one winner this time!

The order of call is the same for all the topics, so you can play 'mix and match' games with different topics. If you decide to do so, make sure that the four different teams are evenly spread.

Different ways of playing/ideas

◆ Call the words from the call sheet in Welsh. Start anywhere, but make a note of where you started either on a photocopy of the call sheet or on a separate sheet of paper. Alternatively, get a child to do the calling. Assist him/her with the more difficult words.

◆ The children take it in turns to call out an item from their own board in Welsh. When they call a word, they colour their own picture and everybody who has that picture says '*diolch*' and colours their picture. Then the child sitting next to the caller says the next word, etc. This is a very good reading exercise if the 'words only' boards are used. The teacher should make a note of which items have been called on the call sheet.

Call the words in English, and the children have to find the Welsh translation (this can only be played with the 'words only' boards).

Show a picture without saying anything (using the 'words only' boards).

Write a word on the board without saying anything (for 'pictures only' boards).

Instead of using the call sheets, photocopy the boards and cut them up into cards, then pick the cards out of a hat. The pupils could take turns to pick a card and call out the word.

Ask the children to colour the pictures before playing and then call the words with a colour, eg '*cath goch*'. To keep the game from lasting too long, limit the children to the same two colours. (You can use the two columns on the call sheets to indicate the colour. For example, write B for "blue" at the top of the list of Welsh words and R for "red" at the top of the English word list.)

Give a description of the word in Welsh.

◆ For the number "loto" boards, give sums for the children to work out.

Spell the words.

Give a rhyming word.

Include the word in a sentence eg *siocled; siocled, os gweli di'n dda; ga i siocled, os gweli di'n dda?*

. Make the game last the whole lesson. Give the boards at the beginning and call the words at intervals during the lesson, either on their own or in a sentence.

Give everybody the same board. Each child has to preselect four items by circling or colouring them.

Give the children the blank template board (pages 57) and get them to write/draw their own items/numbers from a list you have given on the board. This can be played with any topic/structures/verbs/grammar.

◆ Make the children repeat the word several times whilst they are colouring.

◆ The children ask a question each time, eg:

✳ Beth sy gyda ti?   What do you have?

✳ Sawl un? Pa rif?   How many? What number?
  Pa rif sy gyda ti?   What number do yo have?

✳ Beth ydy hwn?   What is this?

✳ Beth wyt ti'n fwyta?   What do you eat?

✳ Oes anifail gyda ti?   Do you have an animal?

✳ Beth wyt ti'n wisgo?   What are you wearing?

◆ If you photocopy the boards double-sided, they will last even longer.

Rhifau 1 i 12

Team 1 to win	Start on 2 or 7
Team 2 to win	Start on 1, 3, 4 or 12
Team 3 to win	Start on 3, 5, 7, 10 or 11
Team 4 to win	Start on 5, 7, 8 or 9
All teams to win	Start on 6

These numbers refer to the numbers on the left and right of the grid below.

Tick the white boxes in the grid as you call out the words.

				Winning team												
				2	1	2&3	2	3&4	All	1,3,4	4	4	3	3	2	
1	pump	five														1
2	naw	nine														2
3	un deg un	eleven														3
4	dau	two														4
5	pedwar	four														5
6	un deg dau	twelve														6
7	tri	three														7
8	un	one														8
9	chwech	six														9
10	wyth	eight														10
11	deg	ten														11
12	saith	seven														12
1	pump	five														1
2	naw	nine														2
3	un deg un	eleven														3
4	dau	two														4
5	pedwar	four														5
6	un deg dau	twelve														6
7	tri	three														7
8	un	one														8
9	chwech	six														9

Order of call

Loto! (Bwrdd 1)

Enw _____

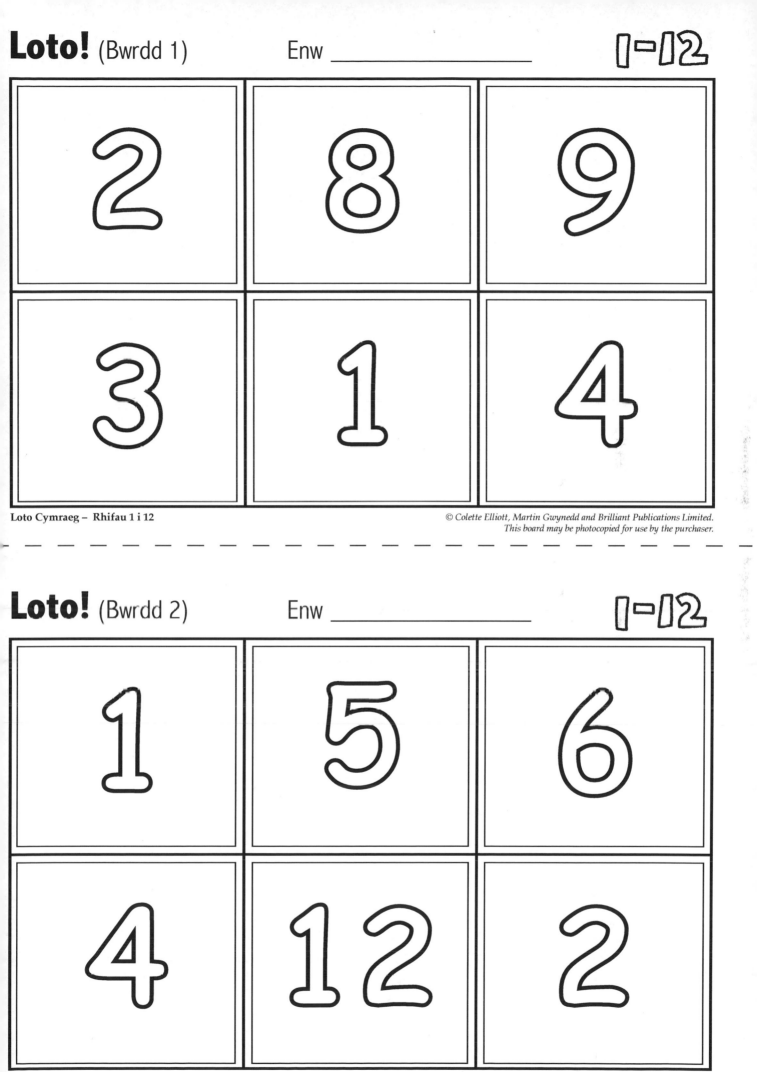

2	8	9
3	1	4

Loto Cymraeg – Rhifau 1 i 12

Loto! (Bwrdd 2)

Enw _____

1	5	6
4	12	2

Loto Cymraeg – Rhifau 1 i 12

Loto! (Bwrdd 3)   Enw _____   1-12

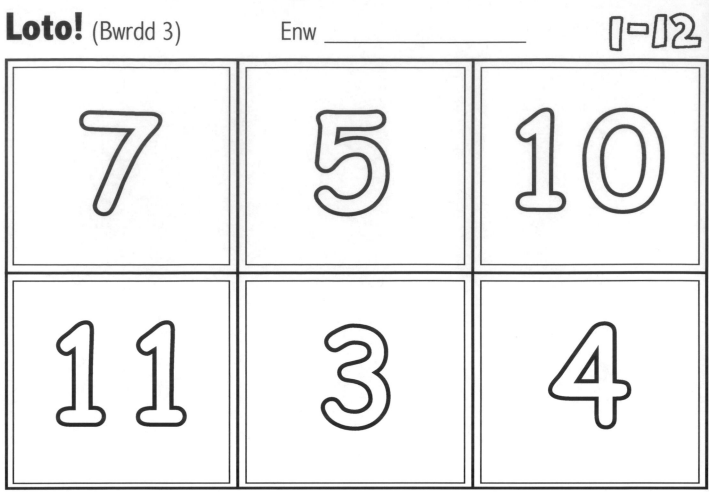

Loto! (Bwrdd 4)   Enw _____   1-12

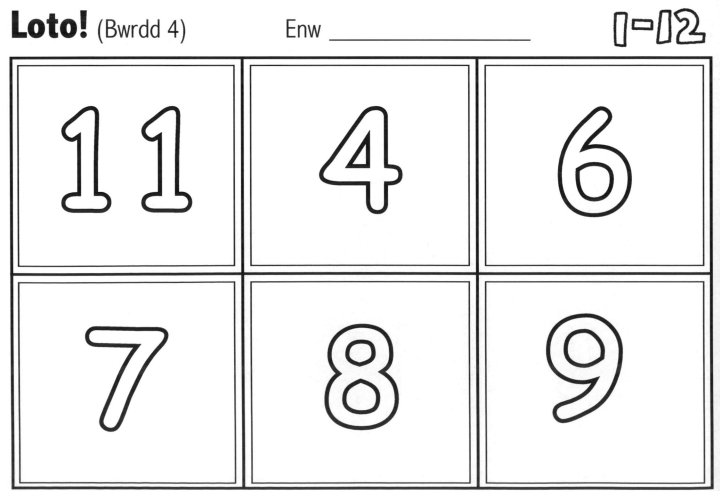

Loto! (Bwrdd 1)

Enw _____

1-12

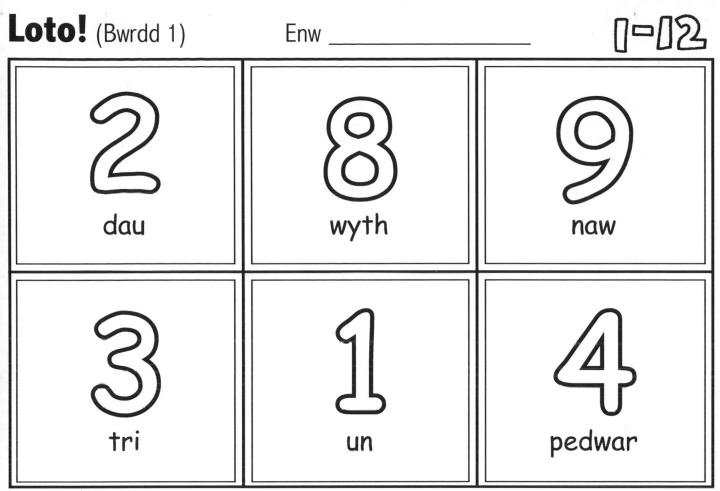

2 dau	**8** wyth	**9** naw
3 tri	**1** un	**4** pedwar

Loto! (Bwrdd 2)

Enw _____

1-12

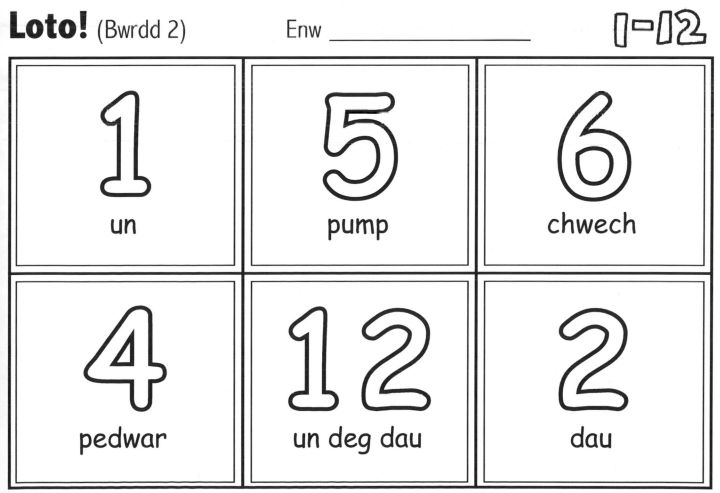

1 un	**5** pump	**6** chwech
4 pedwar	**12** un deg dau	**2** dau

Loto! (Bwrdd 3)   Enw _____   1-12

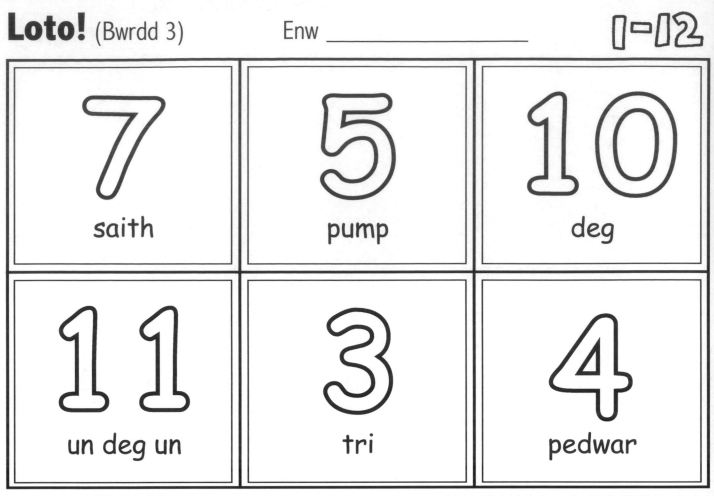

| 7 saith | 5 pump | 10 deg |
| 11 un deg un | 3 tri | 4 pedwar |

Loto! (Bwrdd 4)   Enw _____   1-12

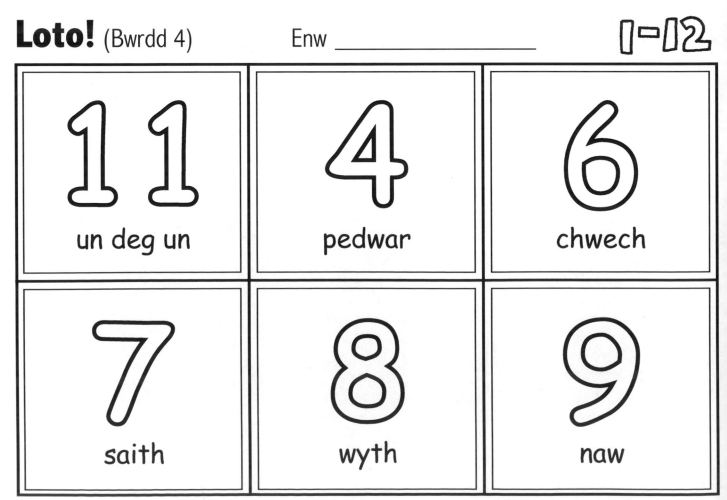

| 11 un deg un | 4 pedwar | 6 chwech |
| 7 saith | 8 wyth | 9 naw |

Loto! (Bwrdd 1)

Enw _____

1-12

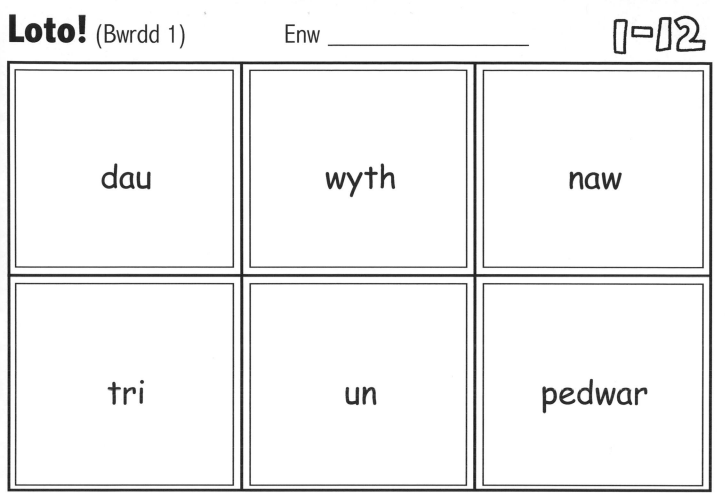

dau	wyth	naw
tri	un	pedwar

Loto! (Bwrdd 2)

Enw _____

1-12

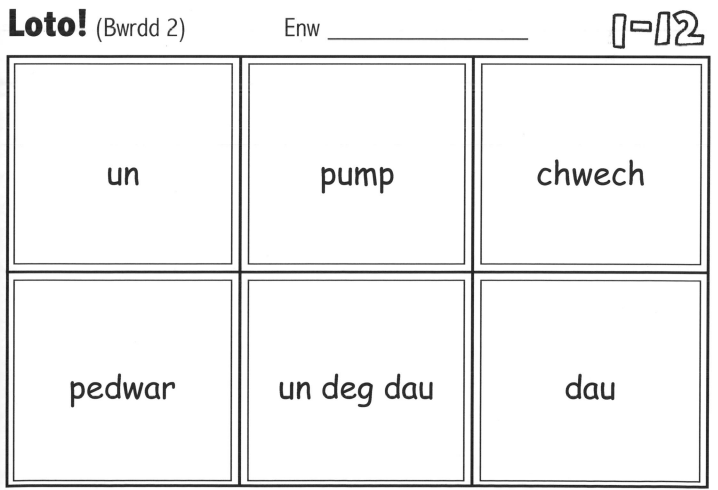

un	pump	chwech
pedwar	un deg dau	dau

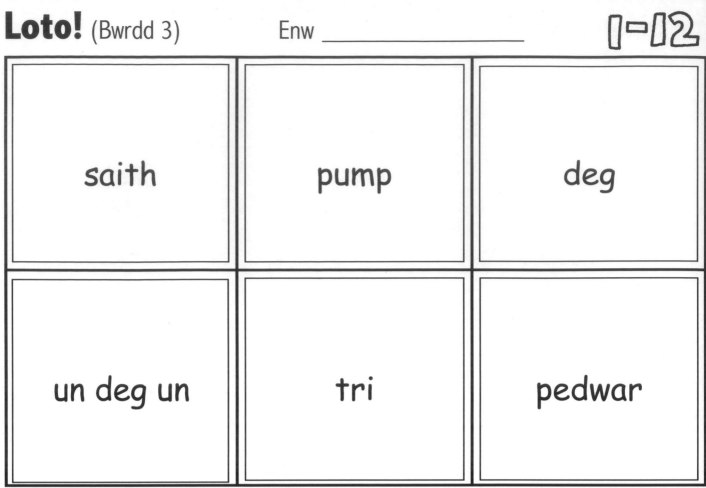

saith	pump	deg
un deg un	tri	pedwar

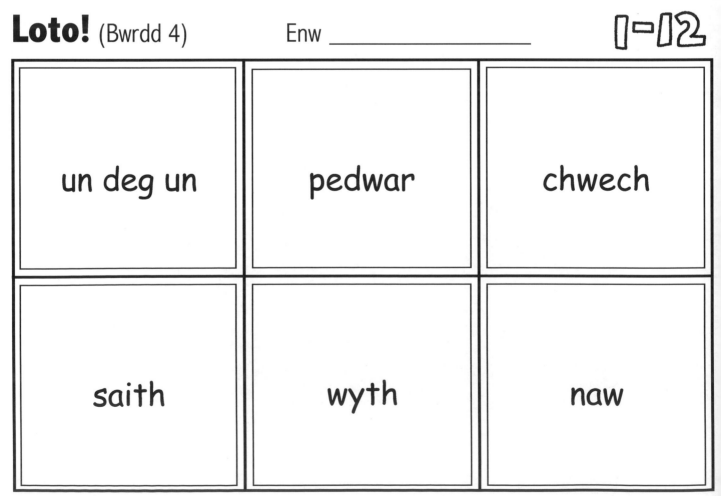

un deg un	pedwar	chwech
saith	wyth	naw

Rhifau 1 i 60

1-60

Team 1 to win	Start on 2 or 7
Team 2 to win	Start on 1, 3, 4 or 12
Team 3 to win	Start on 3, 5, 7, 10 or 11
Team 4 to win	Start on 5, 7, 8 or 9
All teams to win	Start on 6

These numbers refer to the numbers on the left and right of the grid below.

Tick the white boxes in the grid as you call out the words.

					Winning team										
				2	1	2&3	2	3&4	All	1,3,4	4	4	3	3	2	
1	dau ddeg chwech	twenty-six														1
2	saith	seven														2
3	chwech deg	sixty														3
4	tri deg pump	thirty-five														4
5	pump deg wyth	fifty-eight														5
6	pedwar deg un	forty-one														6
7	un deg pump	fifteen														7
8	pump deg	fifty														8
9	un deg dau	twelve														9
10	pedwar deg dau	forty-two														10
11	tri deg pedwar	thirty-four														11
12	un deg naw	nineteen														12
1	dau ddeg chwech	twenty-six														1
2	saith	seven														2
3	chwech deg	sixty														3
4	tri deg pump	thirty-five														4
5	pump deg wyth	fifty-eight														5
6	pedwar deg un	forty-one														6
7	un deg pump	fifteen														7
8	pump deg	fifty														8
9	un deg dau	twelve														9

Order of call

© Colette Elliott, Martin Gwynedd and Brilliant Publications Limited.

Loto! (Bwrdd 1)   Enw _____   1-60

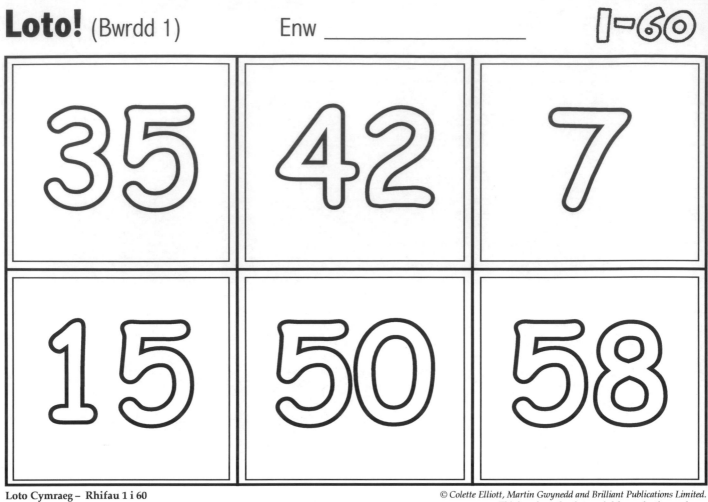

35 | 42 | 7
15 | 50 | 58

Loto Cymraeg – Rhifau 1 i 60

Loto! (Bwrdd 2)   Enw _____   1-60

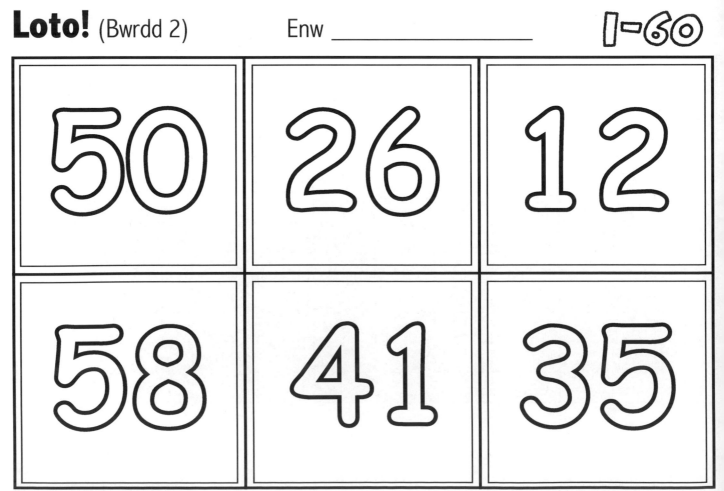

50 | 26 | 12
58 | 41 | 35

Loto! (Bwrdd 3)

Enw _____

1-60

19	26	34
60	15	58

Loto! (Bwrdd 4)

Enw _____

1-60

60	58	12
19	42	7

Loto! (Bwrdd 1)

Enw _____

1-60

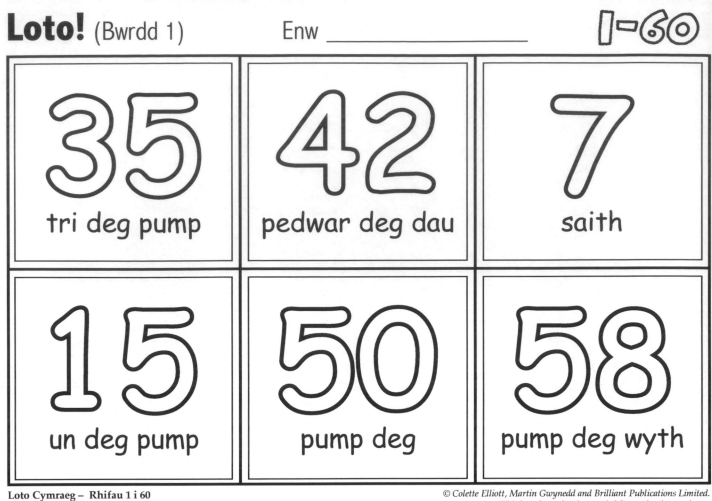

35	42	7
tri deg pump	pedwar deg dau	saith
15	50	58
un deg pump	pump deg	pump deg wyth

Loto Cymraeg – Rhifau 1 i 60

Loto! (Bwrdd 2)

Enw _____

1-60

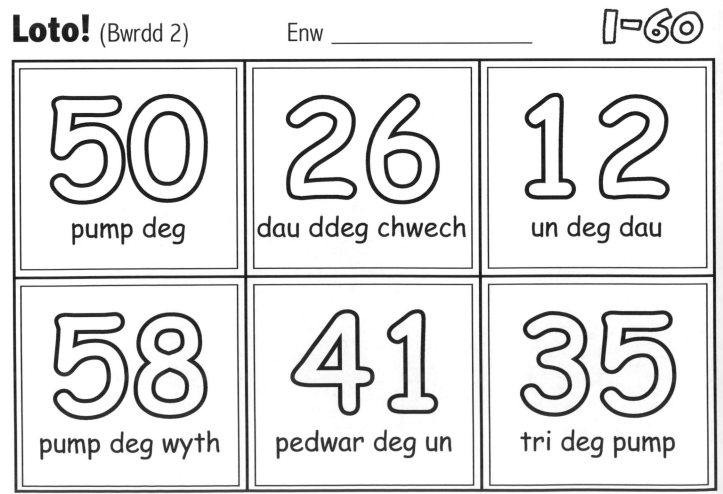

50	26	12
pump deg	dau ddeg chwech	un deg dau
58	41	35
pump deg wyth	pedwar deg un	tri deg pump

Loto! (Bwrdd 3)

1-60

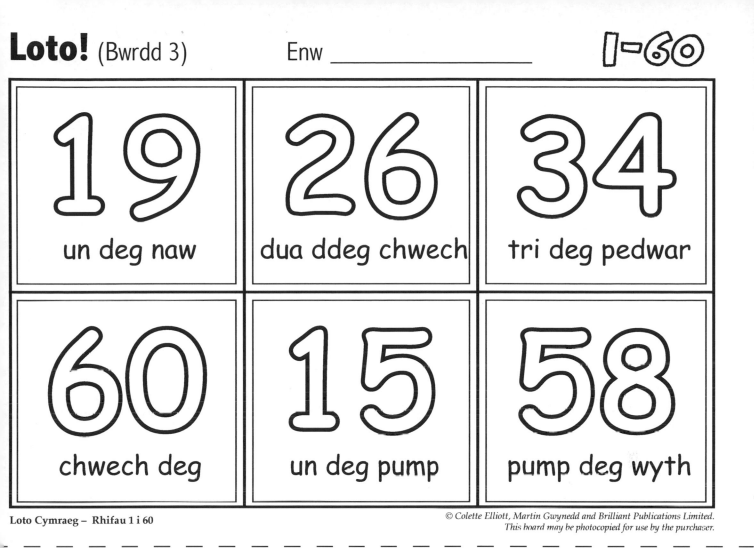

19 un deg naw	**26** dua ddeg chwech	**34** tri deg pedwar
60 chwech deg	**15** un deg pump	**58** pump deg wyth

Loto Cymraeg – Rhifau 1 i 60

Loto! (Bwrdd 4)

1-60

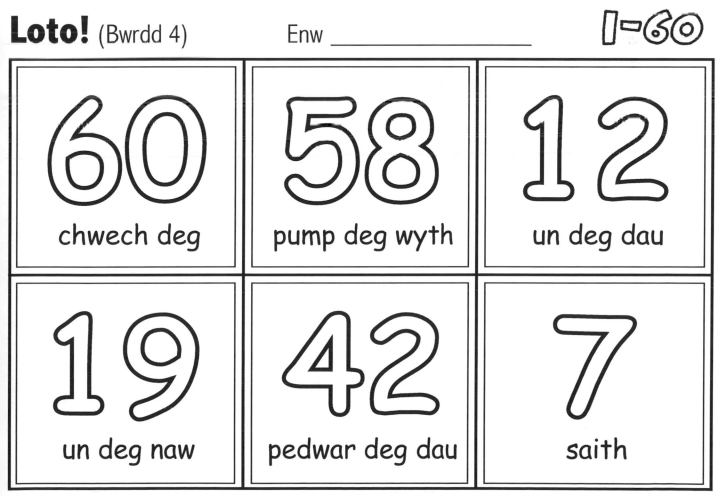

60 chwech deg	**58** pump deg wyth	**12** un deg dau
19 un deg naw	**42** pedwar deg dau	**7** saith

Loto Cymraeg – Rhifau 1 i 60

Enw _____

tri deg pump	pedwar deg dau	saith
un deg pump	pump deg	pump deg wyth

Loto! (Bwrdd 2)

Enw _____

1-60

pump deg	dau ddeg chwech	un deg dau
pump deg wyth	pedwar deg un	tri deg pump

Loto! (Bwrdd 3) Enw _____ 1-60

un deg naw	dau ddeg chwech	tri deg pedwar
chwech deg	un deg pump	pump deg wyth

Loto! (Bwrdd 4) Enw _____ 1-60

chwech deg	pump deg wyth	un deg dau
un deg naw	pedwar deg dau	saith

Anifeiliaid

Team 1 to win	Start on 2 or 7
Team 2 to win	Start on 1, 3, 4 or 12
Team 3 to win	Start on 3, 5, 7, 10 or 11
Team 4 to win	Start on 5, 7, 8 or 9
All teams to win	Start on 6

These numbers refer to the numbers on the left and right of the grid below.

Tick the white boxes in the grid as you call out the words.

				Winning team												
				2	1	2&3	2	3&4	All	1,3,4	4	4	3	3	2	
1	mochyn	pig														1
2	llygoden	mouse														2
3	mochyn gini	guinea pig														3
4	buwch	cow														4
5	bochdew	hamster														5
6	ceffyl	horse														6
7	cwningen	rabbit														7
8	cath	cat														8
9	ci	dog														9
10	pysgodyn aur	goldfish														10
11	hwyaden	duck														11
12	iâr	hen														12
1	mochyn	pig														1
2	llygoden	mouse														2
3	mochyn gini	guinea pig														3
4	buwch	cow														4
5	bochdew	hamster														5
6	ceffyl	horse														6
7	cwningen	rabbit														7
8	cath	cat														8
9	ci	dog														9

Order of call

Loto! (Bwrdd 1)

Enw _____

Loto Cymraeg – Anifeiliaid

Loto! (Bwrdd 2)

Enw _____

Loto Cymraeg – Anifeiliaid

Loto! (Bwrdd 3)

Enw _____

Loto! (Bwrdd 4)

Enw _____

Loto! (Bwrdd 1)

Enw _____

Loto! (Bwrdd 2)

Enw _____

Loto! (Bwrdd 3)

Enw _____

iâr

mochyn

hwyaden

mochyn gini

cwningen

bochdew

Loto! (Bwrdd 4)

Enw _____

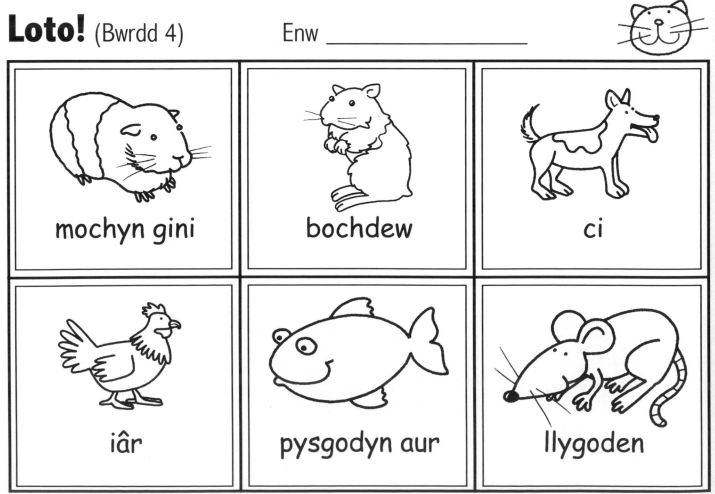

mochyn gini

bochdew

ci

iâr

pysgodyn aur

llygoden

Loto! (Bwrdd 1) Enw _____

buwch	pysgodyn aur	llygoden
cwningen	cath	bochdew

Loto Cymraeg – Anifeiliaid

Loto! (Bwrdd 2) Enw _____

cath	mochyn	ci
bochdew	ceffyl	buwch

Loto Cymraeg – Anifeiliaid

Loto! (Bwrdd 3)   Enw _____

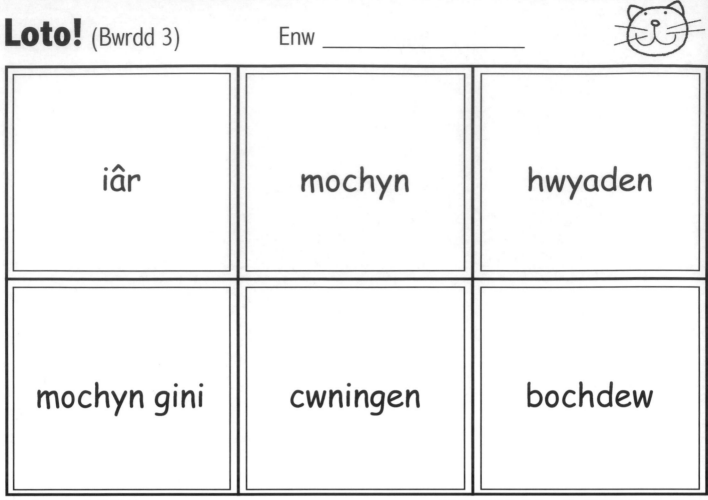

iâr	mochyn	hwyaden
mochyn gini	cwningen	bochdew

Loto! (Bwrdd 4)   Enw _____

mochyn gini	bochdew	ci
iâr	pysgodyn aur	llygoden

Bwyd

Team 1 to win	Start on 2 or 7
Team 2 to win	Start on 1, 3, 4 or 12
Team 3 to win	Start on 3, 5, 7, 10 or 11
Team 4 to win	Start on 5, 7, 8 or 9
All teams to win	Start on 6

These numbers refer to the numbers on the left and right of the grid below.

Tick the white boxes in the grid as you call out the words.

				Winning team											
				2	1	2&3	2	3&4	All	1,3,4	4	4	3	3	2	
1	teisen	cake														1
2	afal	apple														2
3	hufen iâ	ice-cream														3
4	caws	cheese														4
5	cyw iâr	chicken														5
6	taten	potato														6
7	llaeth	milk														7
8	ham	ham														8
9	ŵy	egg														9
10	sglodion	chips														10
11	bara	bread														11
12	siocled	chocolate														12
1	teisen	cake														1
2	afal	apple														2
3	hufen iâ	ice-cream														3
4	caws	cheese														4
5	cyw iâr	chicken														5
6	taten	potato														6
7	llaeth	milk														7
8	ham	ham														8
9	ŵy	egg														9

Order of call

Loto! (Bwrdd 1)

Enw _____

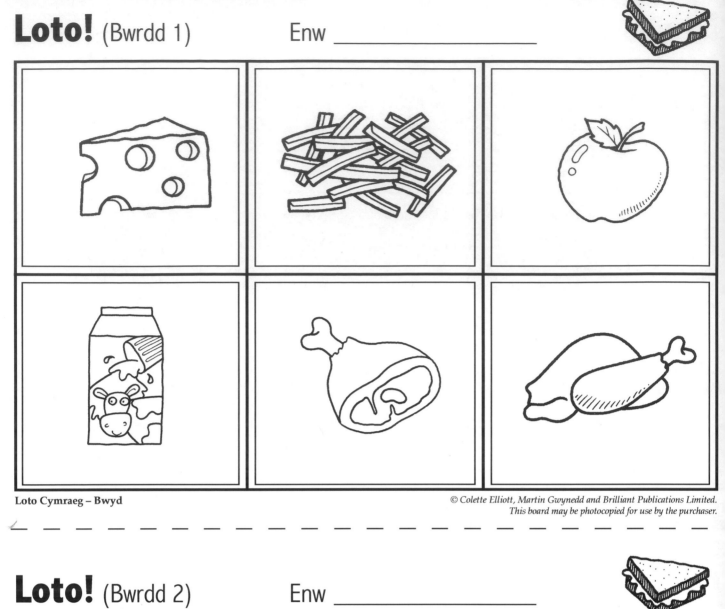

Loto! (Bwrdd 2)

Enw _____

Loto! (Bwrdd 3)

Enw _____

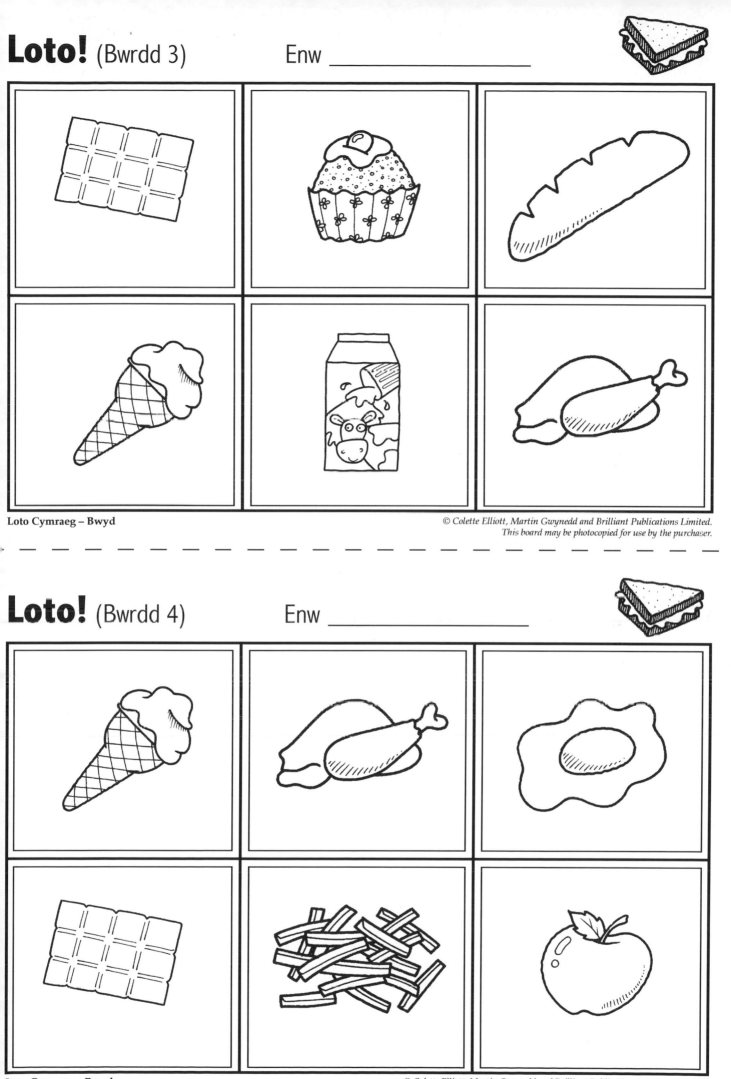

Loto! (Bwrdd 4)

Enw _____

Loto! (Bwrdd 1)

Enw _____

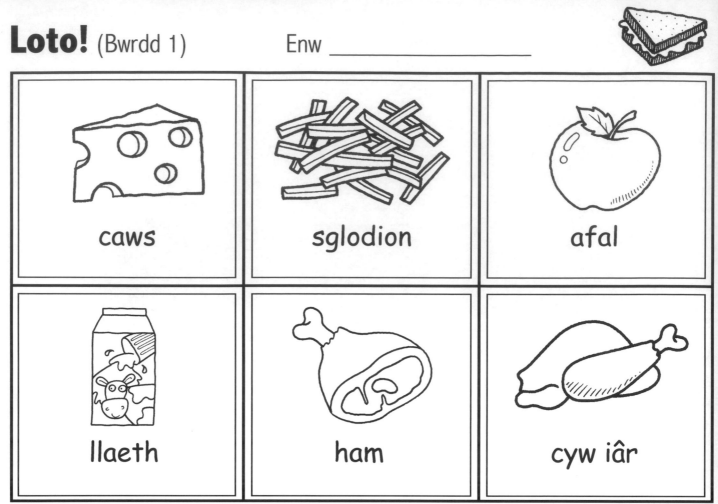

caws

sglodion

afal

llaeth

ham

cyw iâr

Loto Cymraeg – Bwyd

Loto! (Bwrdd 2)

Enw _____

ham

teisen

ŵy

cyw iâr

taten

caws

 Loto Cymraeg – Bwyd

Loto! (Bwrdd 3)

Enw _____

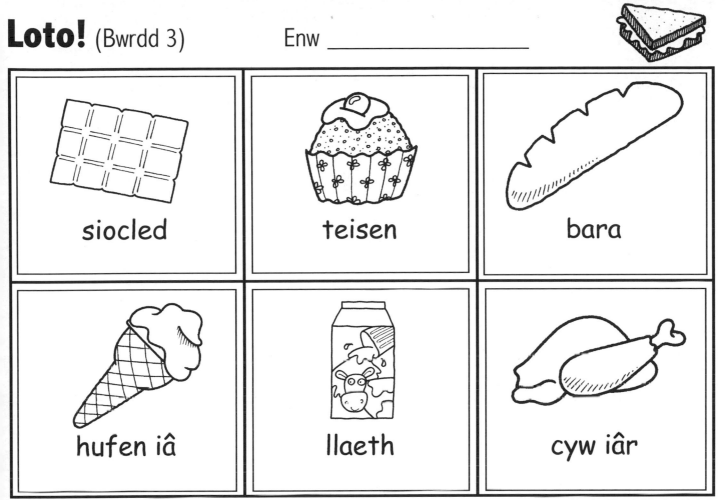

siocled	teisen	bara
hufen iâ	llaeth	cyw iâr

Loto Cymraeg – Bwyd

Loto! (Bwrdd 4)

Enw _____

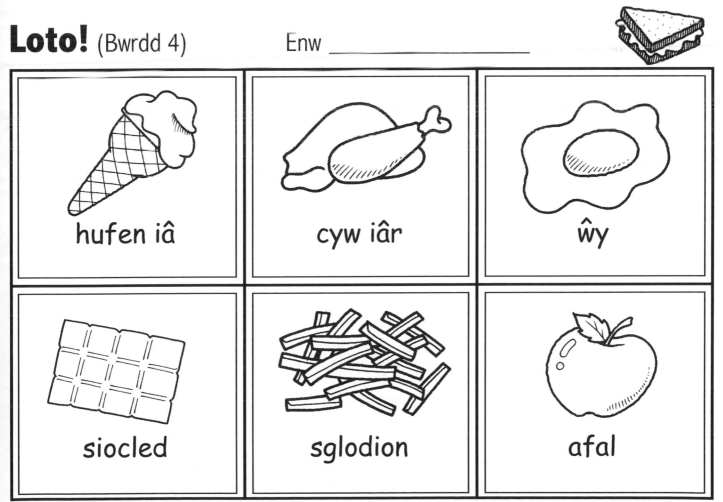

hufen iâ	cyw iâr	ŵy
siocled	sglodion	afal

Loto Cymraeg – Bwyd

Loto! (Bwrdd 1)   Enw _____

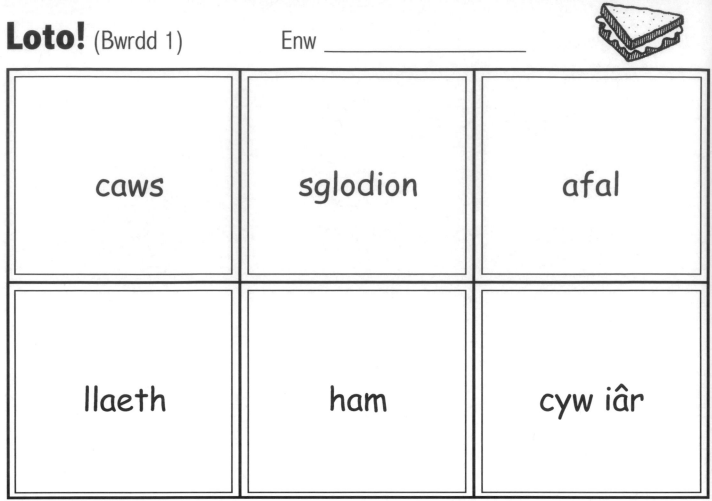

caws	sglodion	afal
llaeth	ham	cyw iâr

Loto! (Bwrdd 2)   Enw _____

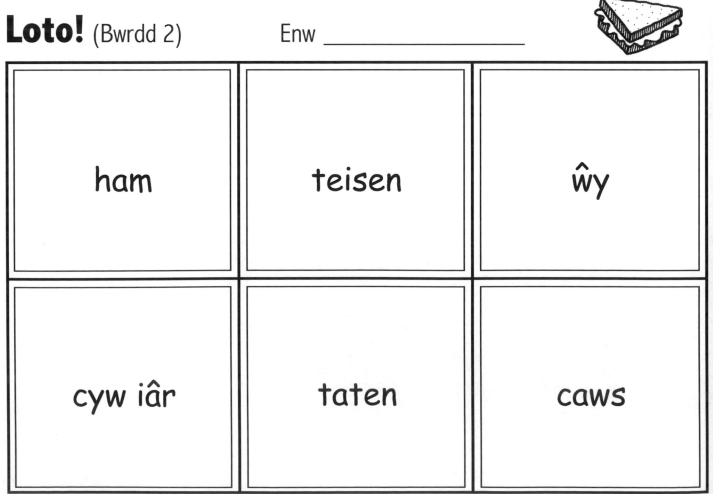

ham	teisen	ŵy
cyw iâr	taten	caws

Loto! (Bwrdd 3)　　　Enw _____

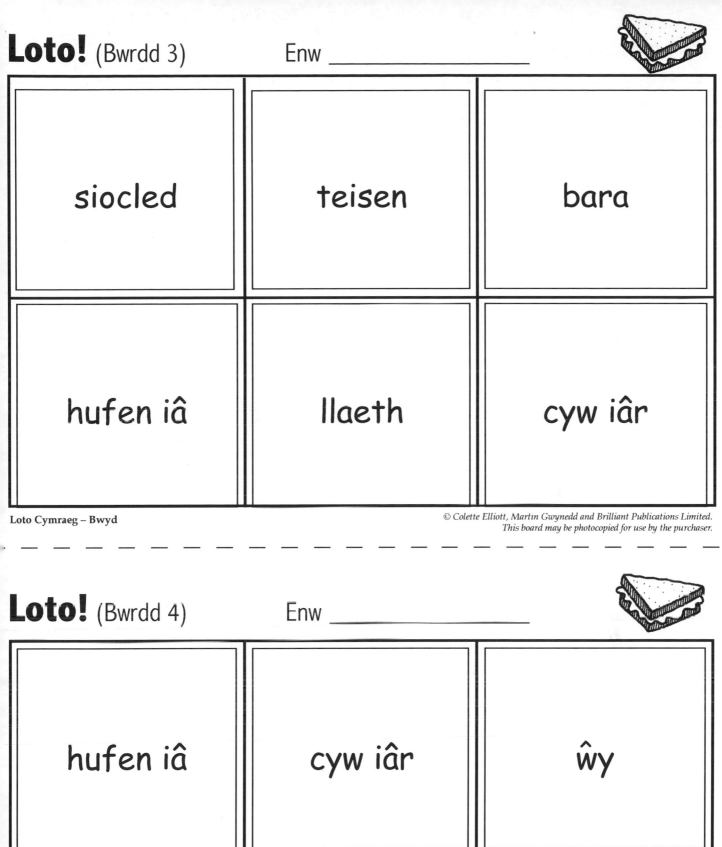

siocled	teisen	bara
hufen iâ	llaeth	cyw iâr

Loto! (Bwrdd 4)　　　Enw _____

hufen iâ	cyw iâr	ŵy
siocled	sglodion	afal

Offer ysgol

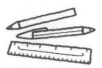

Team 1 to win	Start on 2 or 7
Team 2 to win	Start on 1, 3, 4 or 12
Team 3 to win	Start on 3, 5, 7, 10 or 11
Team 4 to win	Start on 5, 7, 8 or 9
All teams to win	Start on 6

These numbers refer to the numbers on the left and right of the grid below.

Tick the white boxes in the grid as you call out the words.

				Winning team												
				2	1	2&3	2	3&4	All	1,3,4	4	4	3	3	2	
1	llyfr	book														1
2	miniwr	pencil sharpener														2
3	pren mesur	ruler														3
4	bag ysgol	school bag														4
5	siswrn	scissors														5
6	pensil	pencil														6
7	rwber	rubber														7
8	llyfr ysgrifennu	exercise book														8
9	ysgrifbin	pen														9
10	cas pensiliau	pencil case														10
11	cyfrifiannell	calculator														11
12	glud	glue stick														12
1	llyfr	book														1
2	miniwr	pencil sharpener														2
3	pren mesur	ruler														3
4	bag ysgol	school bag														4
5	siswrn	scissors														5
6	pensil	pencil														6
7	rwber	rubber														7
8	llyfr ysgrifennu	exercise book														8
9	ysgrifbin	pen														9

Order of call

Loto! (Bwrdd 1)

Enw _____

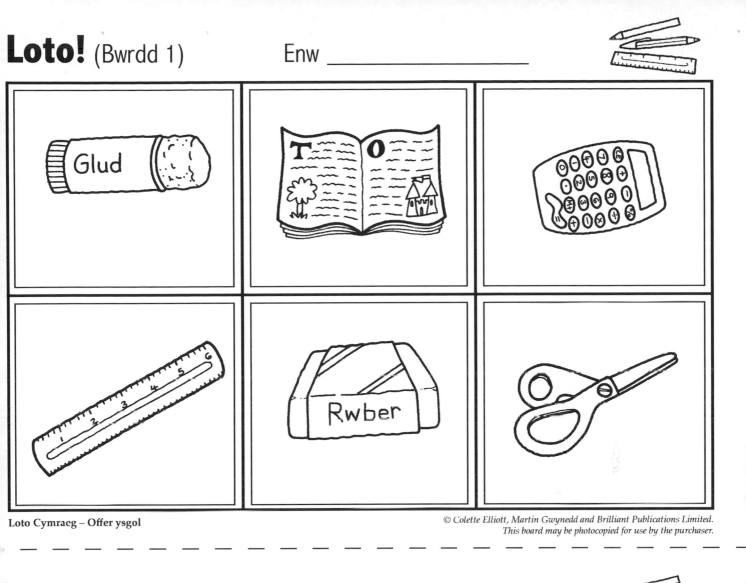

Loto! (Bwrdd 2)

Enw _____

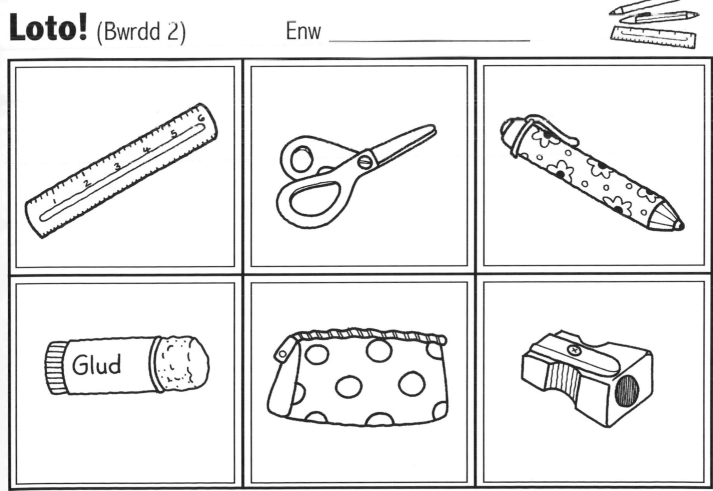

Loto! (Bwrdd 3)   Enw _____

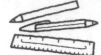

Loto! (Bwrdd 4)   Enw _____

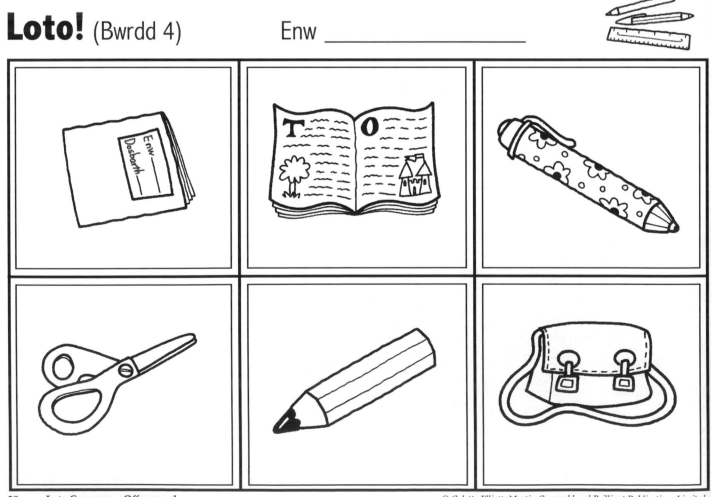

Loto! (Bwrdd 1)   Enw _____

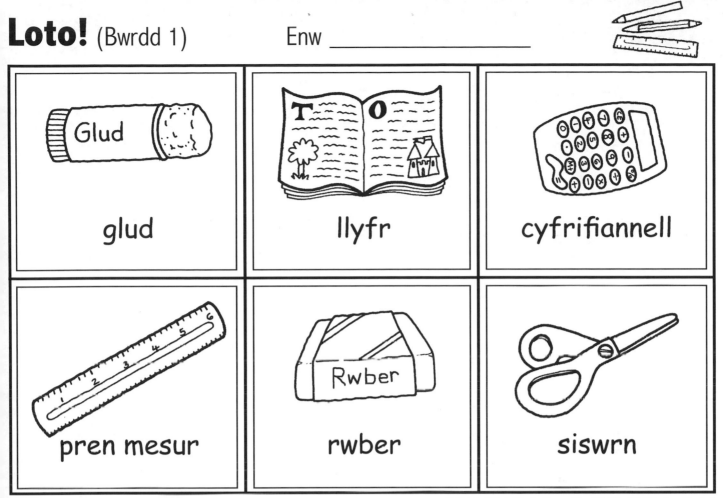

glud	llyfr	cyfrifiannell
pren mesur	rwber	siswrn

Loto! (Bwrdd 2)   Enw _____

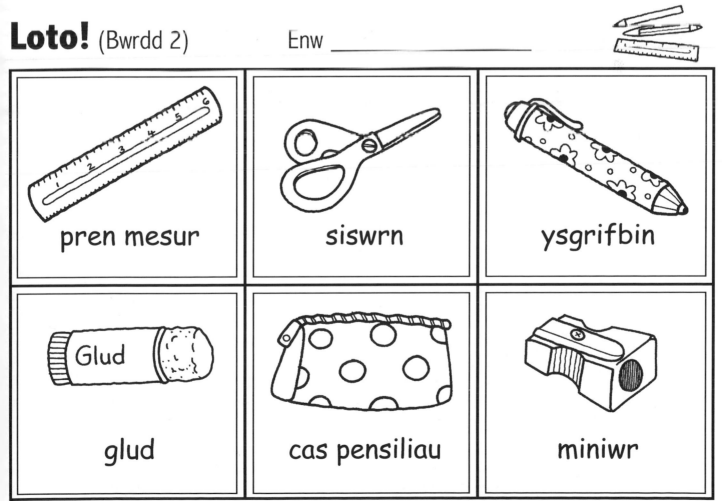

pren mesur	siswrn	ysgrifbin
glud	cas pensiliau	miniwr

Loto! (Bwrdd 3)

Enw _____

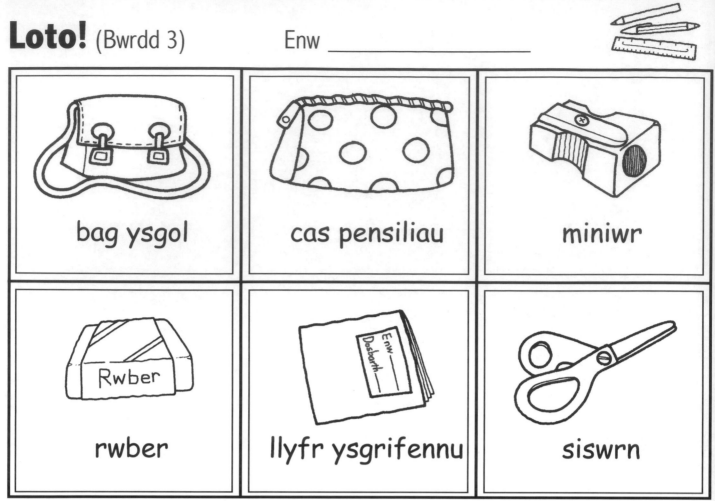

bag ysgol	cas pensiliau	miniwr
rwber	llyfr ysgrifennu	siswrn

Loto! (Bwrdd 4)

Enw _____

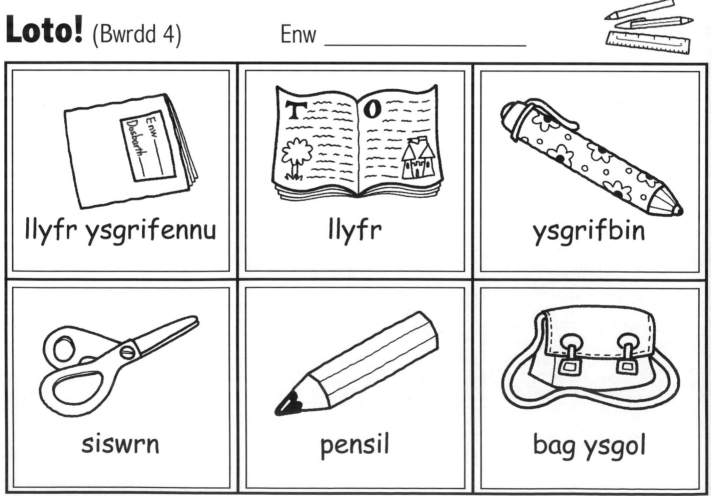

llyfr ysgrifennu	llyfr	ysgrifbin
siswrn	pensil	bag ysgol

Loto! (Bwrdd 1)

Enw _____

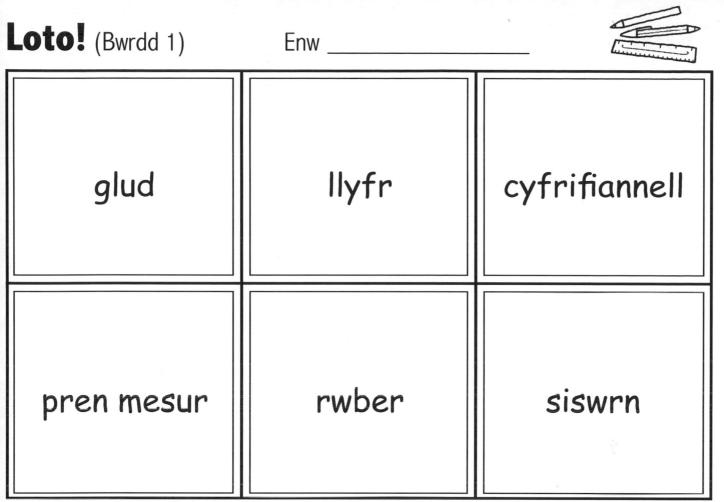

glud	llyfr	cyfrifiannell
pren mesur	rwber	siswrn

Loto Cymraeg – Offer ysgol

Loto! (Bwrdd 2)

Enw _____

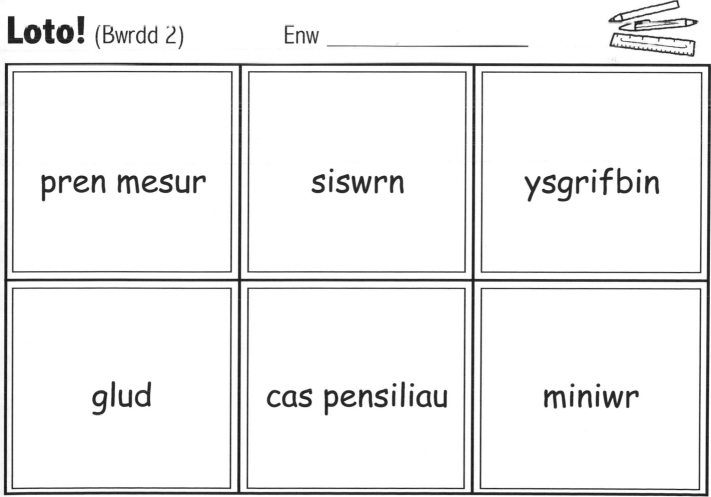

pren mesur	siswrn	ysgrifbin
glud	cas pensiliau	miniwr

Loto Cymraeg – Offer ysgol

Loto! (Bwrdd 3)   Enw _____

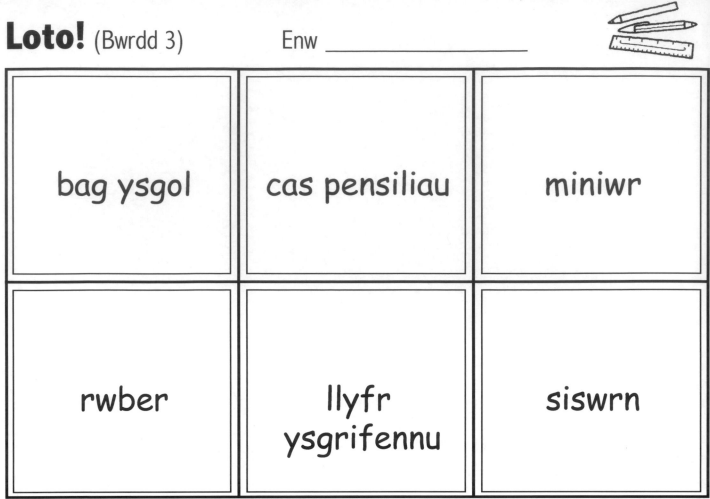

bag ysgol	cas pensiliau	miniwr
rwber	llyfr ysgrifennu	siswrn

Loto! (Bwrdd 4)   Enw _____

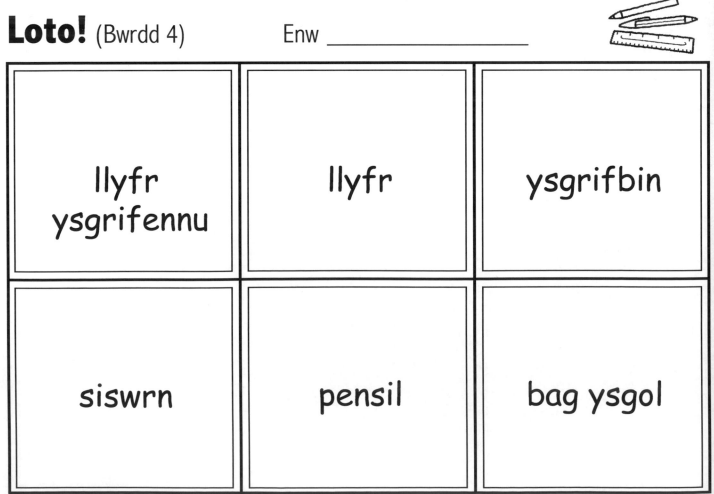

llyfr ysgrifennu	llyfr	ysgrifbin
siswrn	pensil	bag ysgol

Dillad

Team 1 to win	Start on 2 or 7
Team 2 to win	Start on 1, 3, 4 or 12
Team 3 to win	Start on 3, 5, 7, 10 or 11
Team 4 to win	Start on 5, 7, 8 or 9
All teams to win	Start on 6

These numbers refer to the numbers on the left and right of the grid below.

Tick the white boxes in the grid as you call out the words.

				Winning team												
				2	1	2&3	2	3&4	All	1,3,4	4	4	3	3	2	
1	esgidiau	shoes														1
2	jymper	jumper														2
3	ffrog	dress														3
4	trowsus	trousers														4
5	jîns	jeans														5
6	crys T	T-shirt														6
7	het	hat														7
8	sgert	skirt														8
9	crys	shirt														9
10	tci	tic														10
11	sanau	socks														11
12	trowsus cwta	shorts														12
1	esgidiau	shoes														1
2	jymper	jumper														2
3	ffrog	dress														3
4	trowsus	trousers														4
5	jîns	jeans														5
6	crys T	T-shirt														6
7	het	hat														7
8	sgert	skirt														8
9	crys	shirt														9

Order of call

Loto! (Bwrdd 1)   Enw _____

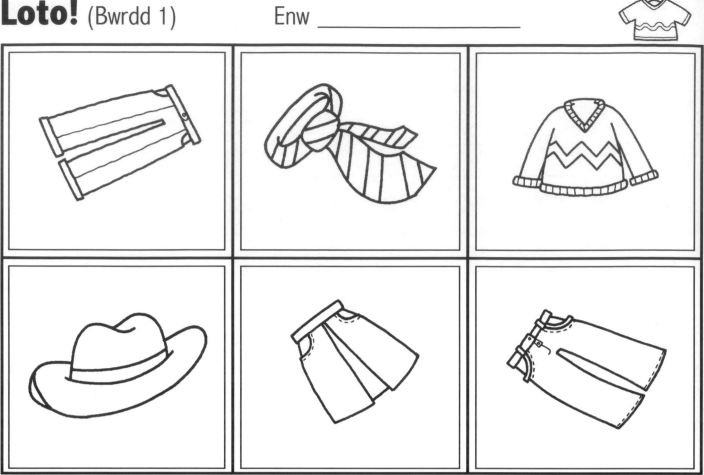

Loto Cymraeg – Dillad

Loto! (Bwrdd 2)   Enw _____

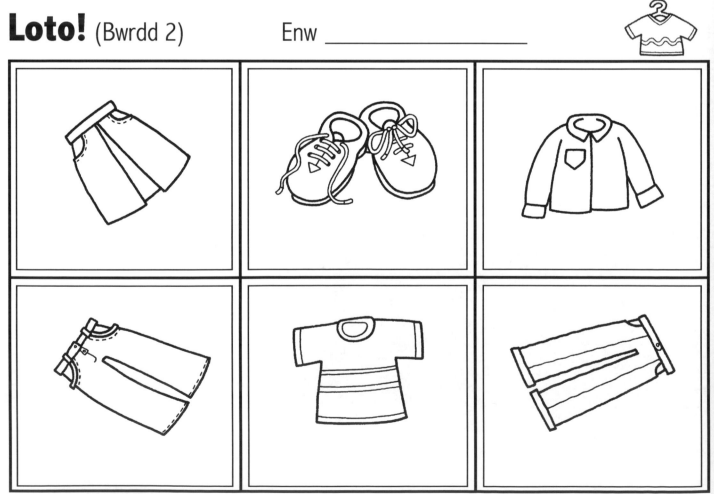

Loto Cymraeg – Dillad

Loto! (Bwrdd 3)

Enw _____

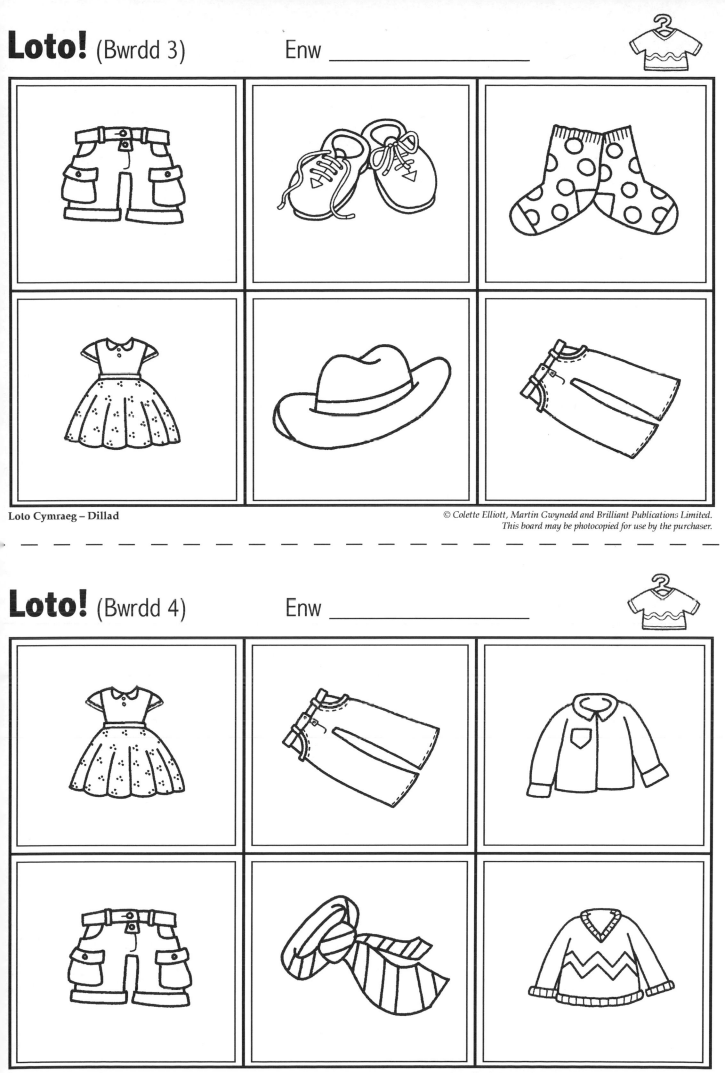

Loto! (Bwrdd 4)

Enw _____

Loto! (Bwrdd 1)

Enw _____

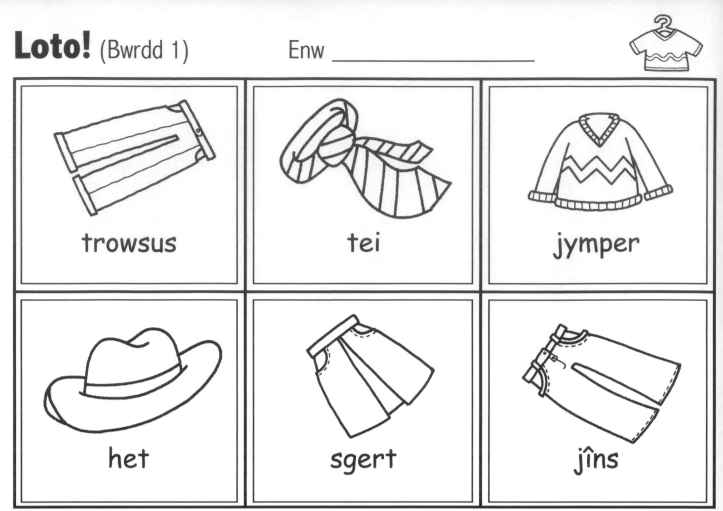

trowsus

tei

jymper

het

sgert

jîns

Loto! (Bwrdd 2)

Enw _____

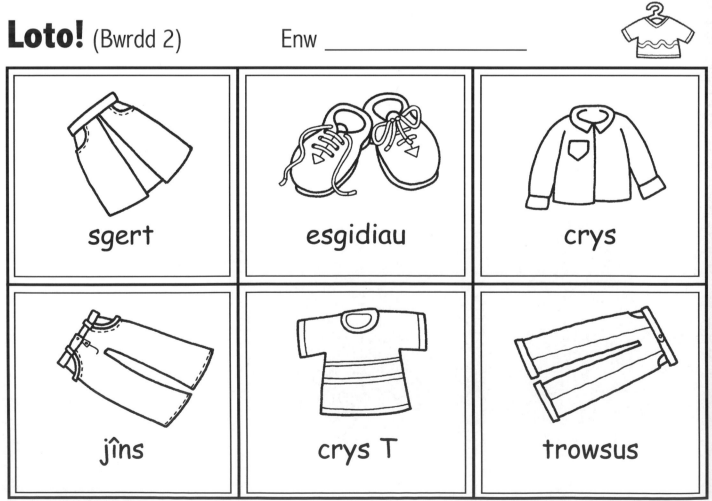

sgert

esgidiau

crys

jîns

crys T

trowsus

Loto! (Bwrdd 3)

Enw _____

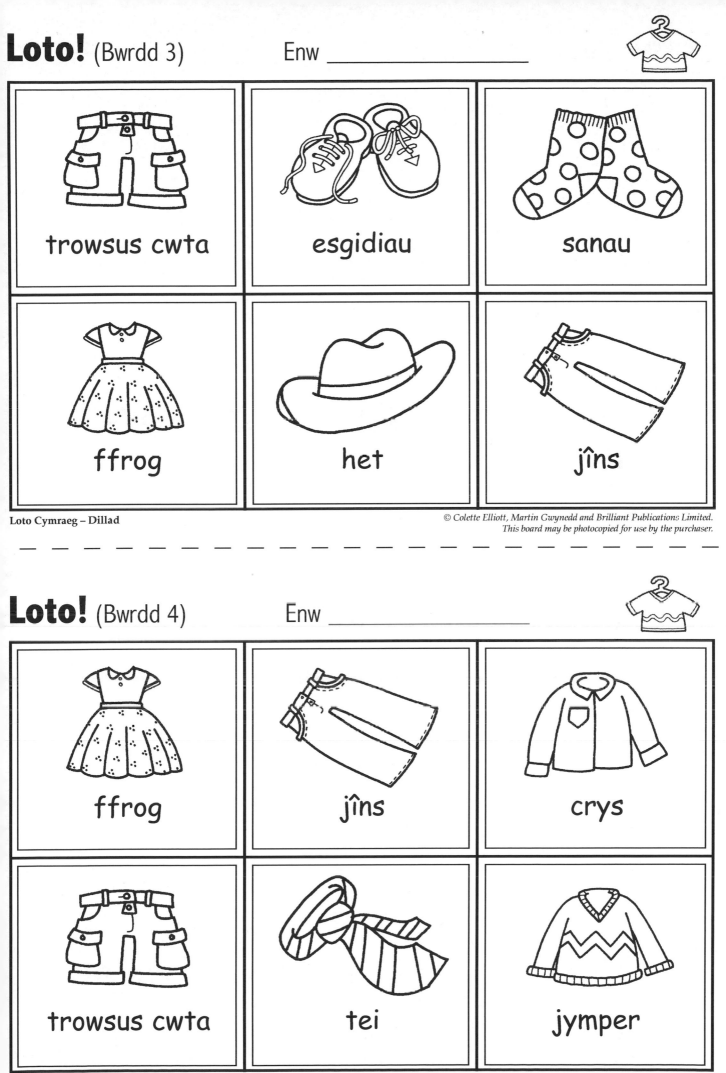

trowsus cwta	esgidiau	sanau
ffrog	het	jîns

Loto Cymraeg – Dillad

Loto! (Bwrdd 4)

Enw _____

ffrog	jîns	crys
trowsus cwta	tei	jymper

Loto Cymraeg – Dillad

Loto! (Bwrdd 1)

Enw _____

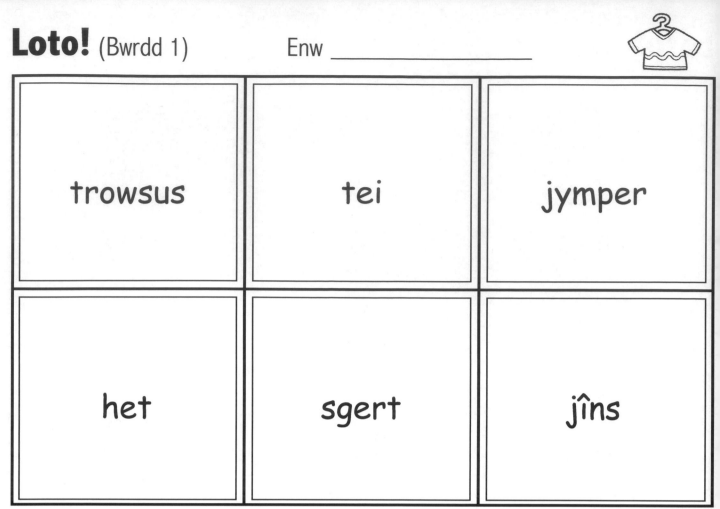

trowsus	tei	jymper
het	sgert	jîns

Loto Cymraeg – Dillad

Loto! (Bwrdd 2)

Enw _____

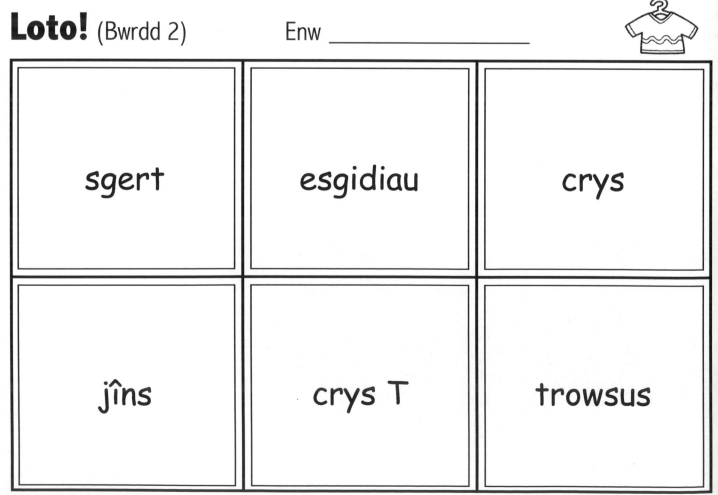

sgert	esgidiau	crys
jîns	crys T	trowsus

Loto! (Bwrdd 3)

Enw _____

trowsus cwta	esgidiau	sanau
ffrog	het	jîns

Loto! (Bwrdd 4)

Enw _____

ffrog	jîns	crys
trowsus cwta	tei	jymper

Nadolig

Team 1 to win	Start on 2 or 7
Team 2 to win	Start on 1, 3, 4 or 12
Team 3 to win	Start on 3, 5, 7, 10 or 11
Team 4 to win	Start on 5, 7, 8 or 9
All teams to win	Start on 6

These numbers refer to the numbers on the left and right of the grid below.

Tick the white boxes in the grid as you call out the words.

				Winning team												
				2	1	2&3	2	3&4	All	1,3,4	4	4	3	3	2	
Order of call	1	celyn	holly													1
	2	twrci	turkey													2
	3	Siôn Corn	Santa Claus													3
	4	dyn eira	snowman													4
	5	Nadolig Llawen	Happy Christmas													5
	6	coeden Nadolig	Christmas tree													6
	7	25 Rhagfyr	25th December													7
	8	seren	a star													8
	9	anrhegion	presents													9
	10	preseb	crib													10
	11	cannwyll	candle													11
	12	carw	reindeer													12
	1	celyn	holly													1
	2	twrci	turkey													2
	3	Siôn Corn	Santa Claus													3
	4	dyn eira	snowman													4
	5	Nadolig Llawen	Happy Christmas													5
	6	coeden Nadolig	Christmas tree													6
	7	25 Rhagfyr	25th December													7
	8	seren	star													8
	9	anrhegion	presents													9

Loto! (Bwrdd 1)

Enw _____

Loto Cymraeg – Nadolig

Loto! (Bwrdd 2)

Enw _____

Loto Cymraeg – Nadolig

Loto! (Bwrdd 3) Enw _____

Loto Cymraeg – Nadolig

Loto! (Bwrdd 4) Enw _____

Loto Cymraeg – Nadolig

Loto! (Bwrdd 1)

Enw _____

dyn eira

preseb

twrci

25 Rhagfyr

seren

Nadolig Llawen

Loto! (Bwrdd 2)

Enw _____

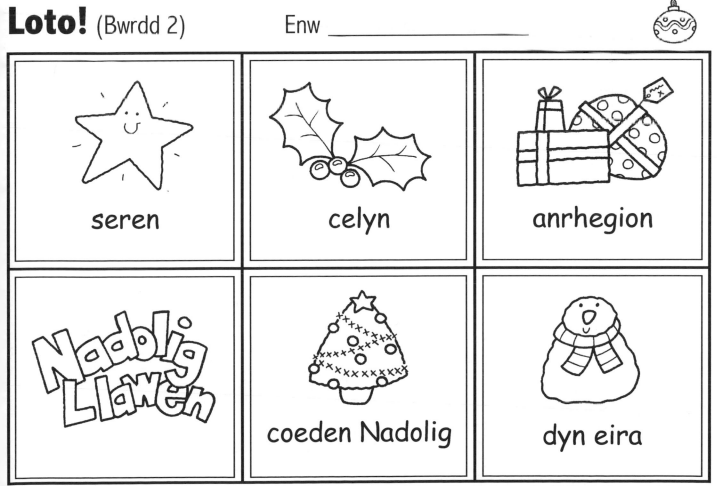

seren

celyn

anrhegion

Nadolig Llawen

coeden Nadolig

dyn eira

Loto! (Bwrdd 3)

Enw _____

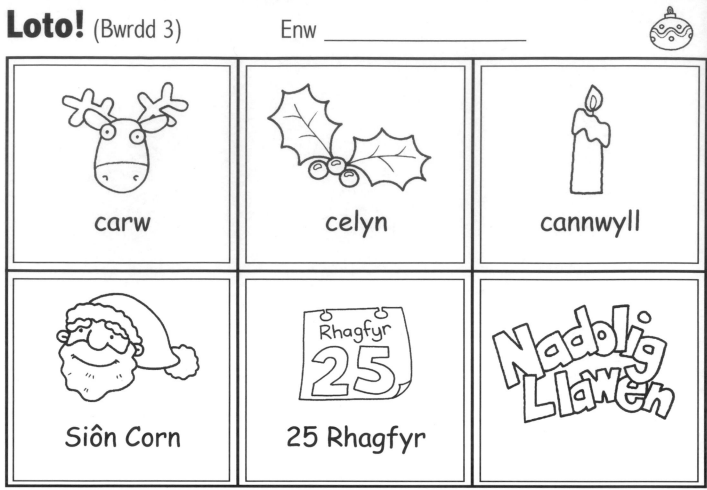

carw	celyn	cannwyll
Siôn Corn	25 Rhagfyr	Nadolig Llawen

Loto! (Bwrdd 4)

Enw _____

Siôn Corn	Nadolig Llawen	anrhegion
carw	preseb	twrci

Loto! (Bwrdd 1)

Enw _____

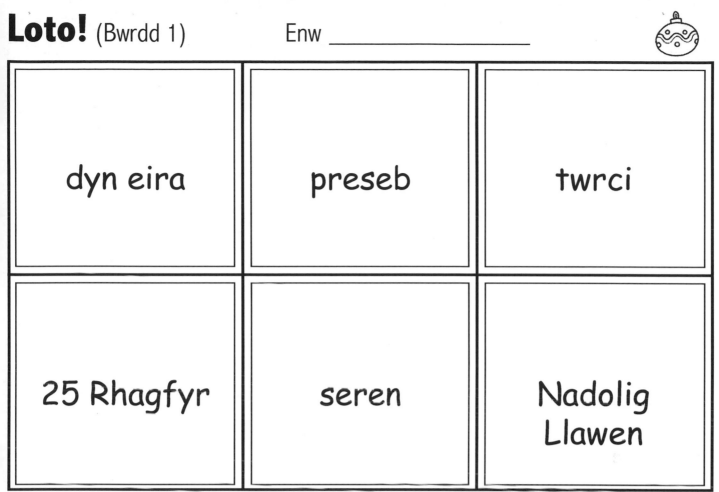

dyn eira	preseb	twrci
25 Rhagfyr	seren	Nadolig Llawen

Loto! (Bwrdd 2)

Enw _____

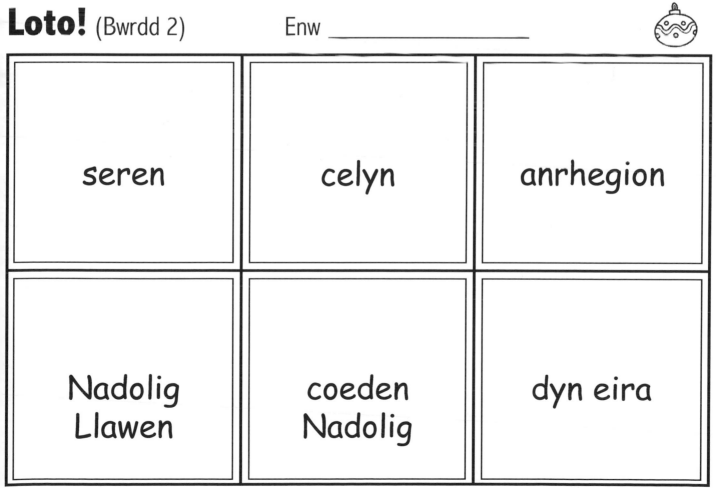

seren	celyn	anrhegion
Nadolig Llawen	coeden Nadolig	dyn eira

Enw _____

carw	celyn	cannwyll
Siôn Corn	25 Rhagfyr	Nadolig Llawen

Loto Cymraeg – Nadolig

Loto! (Bwrdd 4)

Enw _____

Siôn Corn	Nadolig Llawen	anrhegion
carw	preseb	twrci

Loto! (Bwrdd   )   Enw _____

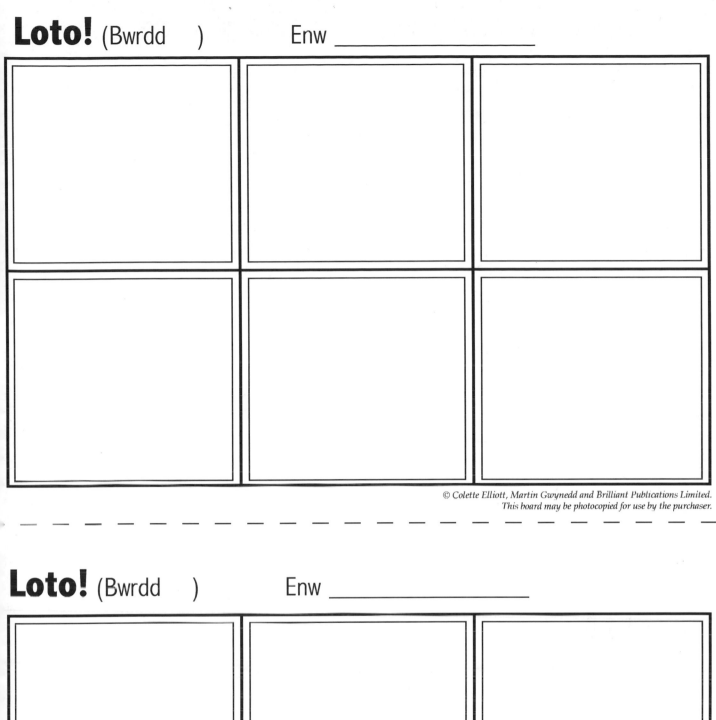

Loto! (Bwrdd   )   Enw _____

List of vocabulary used in the games

Rhifau 1 i 12

un	1
dau	2
tri	3
pedwar	4
pump	5
chwech	6
saith	7
wyth	8
naw	9
deg	10
un deg un	11
un deg dau	12

Rhifau 1 i 60

saith	7
un deg dau	12
un deg pump	15
un deg naw	19
dau ddeg chwech	26
tri deg pedwar	34
tri deg pump	35
pedwar deg un	41
pedwar deg dau	42
pump deg	50
pump deg wyth	58
chwech deg	60

Anifeiliaid

hwyaden	duck
cath	cat
ceffyl	horse
ci	dog
mochyn	pig
mochyn gini	Guinea pig
bochdew	hamster
cwningen	rabbit
pysgodyn aur	goldfish
iâr	hen
llygoden	mouse
buwch	cow

Bwyd

siocled	chocolate
sglodion	chips
caws	cheese
teisen	cake
hufen iâ	ice-cream
ŵy	egg
bara	bread
cyw iâr	chicken

afal	apple
ham	ham
taten	potato
llaeth	milk

Offer ysgol

glud	glue stick
llyfr ysgrifennu	exercise book
cyfrifiannell	calculator
bag ysgol	school bag
siswrn	scissors
pensil	pencil
rwber	rubber
llyfr	book
pren mesur	ruler
ysgrifbin	pen
miniwr	pencil sharpener
cas pensiliau	pencil case

Dillad

het	hat
sanau	socks
esgidiau	shoes
crys	shirt
tei	tie
jîns	pair of jeans
ffrog	dress
trowsus	pair of trousers
jymper	jumper
sgert	skirt
trowsus cwta	pair of shorts
crys T	T-shirt

Nadolig

celyn	holly
twrci	turkey
Siôn Corn	Santa Claus
Nadolig Llawen	Happy Christmas
coeden Nadolig	Christmas tree
25 Rhagfyr	25th December
seren	star
anrhegion	presents
preseb	crib
cannwyll	candle
carw	reindeer
dyn eira	snowman